TEENS IN RUSSIA

Teens in Russia

by Jessica Smith

Content Adviser: Natalia Olshanskaya, Ph.D.,
Associate Professor of Russian,
Department of Modern Languages
and Literatures, Kenyon College

Reading Adviser: Peggy Ballard, Ph.D.,
Department of Educational Studies,
Minnesota State University, Mankato

Compass Point Books ◈ Minneapolis, Minnesota

Compass Point Books
3109 West 50th Street, #115
Minneapolis, MN 55410

Editor: Shelly Lyons
Designers: The Design Lab and Jaime Martens
Page Production: Bobbie Nuytten
Photo Researchers: The Design Lab and Svetlana Zhurkin
Geographic Researcher: Lisa Thornquist, Ph.D.
Cartographer: XNR Productions, Inc.
Library Consultant: Kathleen Baxter

Art Director: Jaime Martens
Creative Director: Keith Griffin
Editorial Director: Carol Jones
Managing Editor: Catherine Neitge

Library of Congress Cataloging-in-Publication Data
Smith, Jessica.
Teens in Russia / by Jessica Smith.
p. cm.—(Global connections)
Includes bibliographical references and index.
ISBN-13: 978-0-7565-2065-6 (library binding)
ISBN-10: 0-7565-2065-7 (library binding)
ISBN-13: 978-0-7565-2073-1 (paperback)
ISBN-10: 0-7565-2073-8 (paperback)
1. Russia (Federation)—Social life and customs—Juvenile literature. 2. Teenagers—Russia (Federation)—Social life and customs—Juvenile literature. 3. Russia (Federation)—Social conditions—1991—Juvenile literature. 4. Teenagers—Russia (Federation)—
Social conditions—21st century—Juvenile literature. I. Title. II. Series.
DK510.762.S64 2006
305.2350947—dc22   2006005301

Visit Compass Point Books on the Internet at www.compasspointbooks.com
or e-mail your request to custserv@compasspointbooks.com.

Table of Contents

8 | Introduction

CHAPTER 1
10 | Post-Soviet School Days

CHAPTER 2
20 | Daily Routines

CHAPTER 3
36 | Fast Friends, Forever Family

CHAPTER 4
42 | A Full Year of Festivities

CHAPTER 5
58 | Teens at Work

CHAPTER 6
66 | Russia is Never Boring!

82 | Looking Ahead

84 At a Glance

86 Historical Timeline

89 Glossary

90 Additional Resources

91 Source Notes

92 Select Bibliography

94 Index

96 Author & Content
   Adviser Bios

96 Image Credits

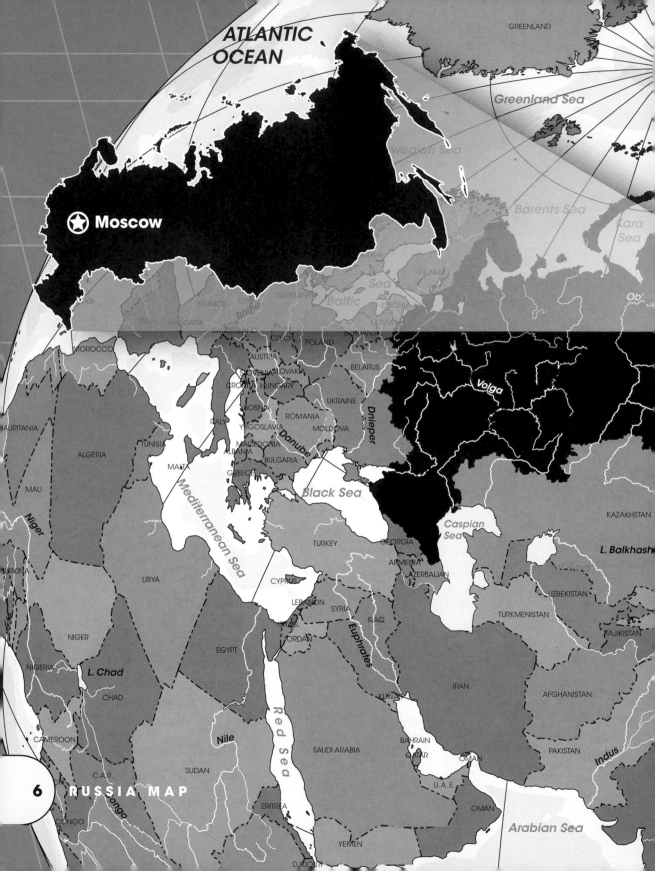

ATLANTIC
OCEAN

GREENLAND

Greenland Sea

wegian Sea

Barents Sea

Kara Sea

⊛ Moscow

Volga

DEN

FINLAND

Baltic Sea

GERMANY

Rhine

FRANCE

LUX

SPAIN

ANDORRA

SWITZERLAND

CZECH

POLAND

BELARUS

AUSTRIA

SLOVENIA SLOVAKIA

CROATIA HUNGARY

UKRAINE

Dnieper

MOROCCO

nds

ITALY

YUGOSLAVIA

ROMANIA

MOLDOVA

BOSN

Danube

MAURITANIA

TUNISIA

MACEDONIA

ALBANIA

BULGARIA

MALTA

GREECE

KAZAKHSTAN

ALGERIA

MALI

Mediterranean Sea

Black Sea

Caspian Sea

TURKEY

GEORGIA

L. Balkhash

CYPRUS

ARMENIA

AZERBAIJAN

Niger

LEBANON

UZBEKISTAN

LIBYA

SYRIA

IRAQ

TURKMENISTAN

ISRAEL

JORDAN

TAJIKISTAN

Euphrates

KUWAIT

NIGER

EGYPT

IRAN

AFGHANISTAN

Indus

NIGERIA

L. Chad

Nile

Red Sea

BAHRAIN

QATAR

PAKISTAN

RKINA

OMAN

CHAD

U. A. E.

CAMEROON

SAUDI ARABIA

Congo

C.A.R.

SUDAN

OMAN

ERITREA

Arabian Sea

YEMEN

DJIBOUTI

ARCTIC OCEAN

Chukchi Sea

Bering Sea

Laptev Sea

Lena

Aldan

Sea of Okhotsk

Yenisey

RUSSIA

Amur

Angara

Lena

Irtysh

L. Baykal

MONGOLIA

Sea of Japan

JAPAN

NORTH KOREA

SOUTH KOREA

Huang

Yellow Sea

East China Sea

YRGYZSTAN

CHINA

Ganges

BHUTAN

NEPAL

BANGLADESH

Salween

VIETNAM

LAOS

INDIA

MYANMAR

THAILAND

Mekong

Bay of

KAMPUCHEA

South China Sea

INDONESIA

LAUGHTER FLOATS THROUGH THE ROOM AS A RUSSIAN TEEN AND HER FRIENDS SIP CHAI AND GOSSIP ABOUT THE CURRENT MUSIC SCENE. One of the girls attends a vocational school and hopes to become a pastry chef. Another girl attends a special school that will train her to become an architect. A third girl in the group goes to a senior secondary school and hopes to soon gain acceptance into Moscow State University. Although their lives are different, Russian teens find ways to connect, whether it is through common interests in music, sports, school, or work.

Russia is the biggest country in the world in terms of landmass, and it has a population of about 142,893,540 people. Teens make up about 16 percent of the total population. The country, which has a rich and textured past, is immense and varied, and so are the experiences of its residents.

In Russia, the secondary school enrollment rate for females is about 86 percent and for males is 80 percent.

1 Post-Soviet School Days

IMAGINE ONE DAY YOUR HISTORY TEACHER COMES INTO THE CLASSROOM, walking slowly and shuffling papers. This is the day you are supposed to be taking the biggest exam of the year. The teacher's face is grim, and you are thinking that the test is going to be even more difficult than you thought. Then your teacher suddenly faces the class, shrugs, and announces the test is canceled.

If you were a Russian teen in the days leading up to and through the dissolution of the Soviet Union in 1991, this would have been a reality and not a fantasy.

As is the case with many aspects of Russian culture—music, movies, literature, and transportation—the education system is still being sorted out. The communist government, which controlled the country from 1920 to 1991,

Russian students take a trial math exam.

had authority over what could and could not be taught in Russia's schools. During that time, Russia was part of the Union of Soviet Socialist Republics (U.S.S.R.).

For many years, the U.S.S.R.'s communist government failed to disclose a lot of facts to the public, and it wrote history books in ways that made the Soviet government look favorable. Then in 1988, during President Mikhail Gorbachev's period of *glasnost*—when the Russian government adopted a new policy of openness with its people— many historical "facts" the Soviets had included in textbooks were proven false. Russian teens were stunned. Much of what they'd been taught for their entire school careers had been a

lie. Their history exams for that year were canceled.

The post-Soviet era has been difficult for Russian schoolteachers to navigate, but each day school officials come closer to the new goals they have set to get back on track. One of these goals—which Andrei Fursenko, the Russian Minister of Education and Science, set recently—is to make sure that all Russian schools have Internet access by the end of 2007. For Russian teens, this means access to information that will help them achieve their educational dreams.

The biggest change in the school system is the new idea of individuality. Russian teens are now receiving instruction according to their skills and abilities. During Soviet rule, all Russian schools followed a common syllabus. Average teens struggled to keep up with their more advanced classmates. Things were so uniform that even left-handed children were forced to become right-handed.

Today the typical Russian school day begins around 8 A.M., even on Saturdays. Students have about six lessons per day, with short breaks in between. The lessons include subjects such as history, science, foreign language, mathematics, Russian, art, computer science, literature, and specialized courses based on each student's plan of study. Lessons last about 40 minutes each. Midday, students break for a short lunch. If they like, they can eat at the

school cafeteria, which serves meals such as liver and rice, fish and mashed potatoes, sweetened fruit drinks, tea, and sweet rolls for dessert. These lunches cost between 10 and 15 rubles (U.S. 37 to 56 cents). If students don't want to eat at the school cafeteria, they can bring lunches from home or wait to eat until they leave school for the day, usually around 3 P.M.

The school year runs on the quarter system, and there are brief breaks between each quarter. For a week in the fall and spring and the two weeks around New Year's Day and Christmas, students are free from their studies. Summer break starts at the beginning of June and lasts for three months.

When school is in session, students

During spring break, a boy performs bike tricks for his friends in Alexandrovsky Garden in Moscow.

13

know they should show up ready to learn. If they don't, or if they act out, their misbehavior and bad grades are often recorded in their *dnevnik*. The dnevnik is a special notebook students bring with them to school. Important events and deadlines are recorded in it, and students use it to keep track of homework. Teachers use it to record the students' grades and write notes to the students' parents. Parents might take away phone privileges or ground the teen if he or she comes home with a warning from the teacher in the dnevnik.

dnevnik
dnyev-NIK

There are many ways for Russian teens to get to and from school. The price of insuring a car, filling it with gas, and maintaining it can be extremely expensive, so only about 30 percent of Russians own vehicles. Therefore, it is rare to find teens who have cars. Instead, they use the extensive network of public transportation or walk to school. Students can take trolleys or buses that cost around 5 rubles (U.S.19 cents) per ride. Subways are available in Russia's big cities. Trains rumble by on a regular schedule, and students can ride for about 7 rubles (U.S.26 cents). Route taxis, which carry more than one person and follow a specific route, are also available in large cities, with set fares around 9 rubles (U.S.34 cents).

A passenger train stops at a station in Penza, in western Russia.

Moscow Metro

The Moscow Metro is much more than just a way to get around. Constructed during Joseph Stalin's rule, from 1928 to 1953, the Metro's elaborate and ornate underground stations were meant to show travelers how privileged Soviet life was.

Many stations were built with towering columns, archways, and slabs of marble. Some stations are decorated with giant bronze statues of soldiers and farm workers. Other stations are detailed with glittering mosaics. Still others feature elaborate murals and paintings from famous Soviet artists.

The most famous of these metro stations—Novoslobodskaya—is also the most stunning. It features glowing panels of stained glass and a giant mosaic panel entitled *Peace Throughout the World*.

The metro system in Moscow consists of more than 170 stations and 12 lines. On average, the trains transport around 8 million passengers per day.

Teen Scenes

A 13 year-old Russian girl blinks awake at 6:30 A.M. Her alarm rings, signaling the start of another school day, even though it's Saturday. Many Russian schools hold classes six days a week and let out in the mid-afternoon. Her school is no different. She hurries to get ready and dashes out the door of her parents' apartment complex that sits in the heart of the bustling city of Moscow. Around her horns blare and tires squeal. As usual, the traffic is thick and crazy this morning. She doesn't have to worry about traffic on the roads. She is headed to the Metro, where she will board a train and ride it to her school. She could take a bus or a route taxi, but she dreams of becoming a famous artist, so she enjoys waiting in the elaborate mosaic passageways of the Moscow Metro.

At school the teachers present lessons on history, mathematics, science, and English. Finally, when the last bell of the school day sounds, she gathers her books and joins her friends in the hallway.

Later that evening, she helps her mother prepare dinner and then watches her little sister while the adults linger over dessert and tea. Tomorrow she will have the entire day off, and she is excited to go to the park or the movies with her friends.

Meanwhile, in a small village near the Volga River, another 13 year-old Russian girl is waking up for her own school day. Unlike the girl who lives in a big city, this girl lives in a rural area and must wake up much earlier to perform a few light chores before heading off to school. She helps feed her baby brother, washes the breakfast dishes, and makes sure the small animals—a dog, a cat, and several chickens—are fed and watered. She leaves her house, which is small but cozy, and latches the gate to the creaking fence around it. She walks to school, which is also very small and has only a few students in each grade. After 9th grade, students at her school will have the option to attend either a senior secondary school or a specialized trade school.

On lunch break, she walks home for her afternoon meal—soup, a beef patty, and a sweet roll. She washes her dishes and goes back to school to finish her afternoon session. Afterward, she and her friends take a long walk through the village's packed-dirt roads. Some talk about wanting to grow up to work in the city as architects or bankers. Other friends say they want to stay in their small village, marry a suitable partner, raise children, and farm the land.

Tonight her parents are having company, and her mother has asked for her help in the kitchen. She will spend her afternoon making *zakuski*—hors d'oeuvres—with her mother, in order to impress and make their guests feel welcome. Later she will tend to the baby while the adult guests raise their glasses and toast to health, happiness, love, and success.

zakuski
zah-KOOHS-keeh

While uniforms are not required in public schools, a dress code still exists. Russian teens cannot have tattoos that show from underneath clothing. Girls' shirts must cover their stomachs, or they will be sent home to change.

School isn't all seriousness. At the beginning of a school year, there might be dances or talent shows, where classes compete against each other. Students sing songs, recite poems, and give presentations in a competition to see who will be crowned the most talented class. During the school year, there are plenty of school dances or sports games to attend. At the end of the school year, school officials may throw goodbye parties for their students. A student in Penza loves this time of year because of the exciting events that come along with it:

"At the end of the school year, we have an event called 'School Year Summary' with the entertainment program prepared by students, when individual students are recognized for their personal achievements in studies, sports, and for participation in architecture and design expositions."

Students might also put on skits and art shows to display their talents.

Students who have passed their final exams and are graduating from high school participate in a ceremony called Last Bell. In late May, the graduates gather with their peers and teachers to say their goodbyes to each other.

Private schools are now considered the best place for learning because the teachers tend to be paid much higher salaries. Teachers can afford to give more individual attention to students while also getting paid more. Students pay as much as 80,428 rubles (U.S.$3,020) a year to attend private schools, but they are tutored intensely in the study of the English language and other skills critical to success in Russia's changing economy. Of course, no matter what type of school a Russian teen attends, this fact remains: The literacy rate in Russia is nearly 100 percent.

After secondary school, at age 15, Russian teens face a tough choice. There are many options for them to consider. They could attend a *spetsializirovannaya shkola*—a specialized school that gives intensive instruction in foreign languages, math, or sports. Another choice is a *uchilische*—a vocational school that trains students to master a trade, such as plumbing. Yet another choice for teens is to attend a *technikum*—a

spetsializirovannaya shkola
spe-tsee-ah-leeh-ZEEH-rah-vahn-nah-yah SHKOH-lah

uchilische
ooh-CHEEH-leeh-shah

technikum
TEKH-neeh-kum

Russian students often remain together, in the same class, from first grade through graduation. When they finally celebrate Last Bell, they must say goodbye to close friends.

vocational school that offers training in professional careers in areas such as electronics and management. Teens can also choose to go to a traditional *universitet,* the university. Once there, they can engage in a concentrated five-year program that leads to a diploma. A teen interested in going further through school could even plan on attending *aspirantura*—post-graduate study institutions—after graduating from the university.

Of course, before Russian teens graduate, they need to have one last party: prom! Students spend prom night dining at their favorite local restaurants and dancing into the late hours of the night as a DJ spins heavy club beats.

After Russian teens have celebrated prom, they soon march across the graduation stage. In any given year, there may be as many as 75,000 teens participating in graduation ceremonies across the nation.

universitet
ooh-neeh-ver-seeh-TET

aspirantura
ahs-peeh-rahn-TOOH-rah

Tragedy in Beslan

Disaster struck the town of Beslan, Russia, on the first day of school, September 1, 2004. A large group of Chechen terrorists swarmed the school. They herded students and teachers into the gymnasium and locked them inside. The captives were threatened with guns, beaten, and many were even shot. The siege lasted three long days. Russian police finally broke into the gymnasium to free the imprisoned students.

More than 300 civilians were killed, and at least 186 of them were children.

The men who claimed responsibility for the killings said they were trying to send a message. It is reported that they hoped the Belsan siege would cause Russia to grant independence to the Muslim-majority republic of Chechnya. All but one of the terrorists were killed, and the sole survivor was sentenced to life in prison.

After the end of the Beslan siege, grieving members of the community visited the school gymnasium where victims of the siege had been held.

Traffic in Moscow can be a nightmare. There are approximately 3 million vehicles in Moscow already and another 200,000 are added each year.

2 Daily Routines

CITY LIFE CAN BE BUSY, dirty, and crowded. Cars, buses, and trucks pack the streets, and the air fills with noxious fumes caused by jumbled traffic jams. There is never a shortage of noise or movement.

Russian teens like to come home to their cozy homes after a long day of school and work. It's not uncommon to find several generations of a family all living in the same—and relatively small—space. Grandparents, aunts, uncles, and cousins may all share one or two bathrooms and bedrooms. Smaller families of three or four people can live in an apartment that has one room besides the kitchen and bathroom. Most teens share a bedroom with another family member such as a brother or sister.

Sharing housing with

21

extended family makes sense for some Russian families. For instance, if a Russian teen's grandfather had been in the military, his retirement fund might have provided him and his entire family a reasonably priced place to live. Another perk? Free childcare. Grandmothers who no longer hold day jobs can stay at home with the youngest children and tend to them while the parents are at work. In this sense, it's extremely logical for an extended family to live together.

Russian teens not living with three generations of their family might come home each day and climb the stairs up to their apartment in one of the towering complexes that are popular in cities. Still other Russian teens might find themselves relaxing after a long day in

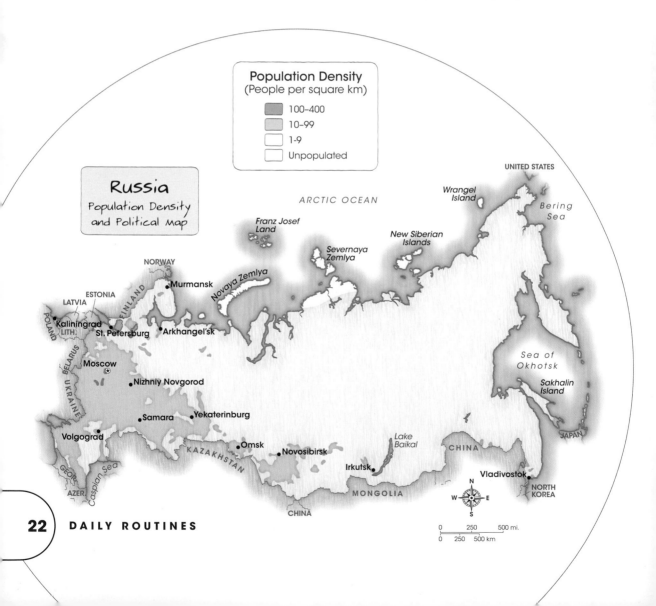

Population Density
(People per square km)

- 100–400
- 10–99
- 1-9
- Unpopulated

Russia
Population Density and Political Map

ARCTIC OCEAN

UNITED STATES

Wrangel Island

Bering Sea

Franz Josef Land

New Siberian Islands

Severnaya Zemlya

NORWAY

Murmansk

Novaya Zemlya

ESTONIA

LATVIA

FINLAND

POLAND

Kaliningrad

LITH.

St. Petersburg

Arkhangel'sk

BELARUS

Moscow

UKRAINE

Nizhniy Novgorod

Samara

Yekaterinburg

Volgograd

KAZAKHSTAN

Omsk

Novosibirsk

Irkutsk

Lake Baikal

Sea of Okhotsk

Sakhalin Island

JAPAN

CHINA

Vladivostok

GEOR.

Caspian Sea

AZER.

MONGOLIA

NORTH KOREA

CHINA

N W E S

0   250   500 mi.
0   250   500 km

According to the latest census, 73 percent of Russians live in urban areas.

their brand new "exclusive" apartments or individual townhouses—but only if their parents are among the Novye Russkie, or "New Russians." The Novye Russkie are those Russians who have become very wealthy since the fall of the Soviet government. They are buying the newest and most decorative housing that is springing up in pockets around St. Petersburg, Moscow, and other cities. These Russians are fashionable and flashy. They have shiny new cars,

expensive clothes from the best fashion houses, and the newest cell phones.

Russians who don't live in a city or its outskirts find themselves in homes in the country, sometimes without running water, gas, or indoor plumbing. A wooden cottage is the common house for country dwellers. At their center, many have beautifully decorated stoves that heat the entire house. Some also contain wooden window frames carved with designs.

Heading to the Dacha

The Russian countryside can have a relaxing, restoring effect on those who spend long hours commuting, working, and playing in the busy cities.

It is common for Russian families to own a *dacha*. These are modest wooden or brick buildings in the countryside. Although they are small and have few comforts of home, the dachas serve a practical purpose. Russians may also keep small gardens on their plot of land, so they can save money on food. Russian teens might have some weeding or harvesting to do at the dacha as part of their regular summer chores.

When they aren't sorting budding vegetables from weeds, Russian teens can enjoy other things about their summer retreat: They can hike, go on long walks in the forest, swim, or ride bicycles. It's certainly a welcome break from the hustle and bustle of the city, but the gardens also serve the important purpose of saving Russian families money. The fruits and vegetables planted at a dacha save a family from having to buy more groceries with its already stretched budget.

dacha
DAH-chah

Dachas commonly have a garden in the yard, and some have greenhouses as well.

Chores

Teen girls and boys often have different chores. Girls are likely to be put in charge of child care and things considered to be typical domestic duties. They stand alongside their mothers and watch them make meals. They stir soups that boil on the stove, mend popped buttons and torn cuffs, and walk their younger siblings to the park.

Teen boys, on the other hand, often take care of the more mechanical or heavy-lifting work. They help their fathers with small home repairs, like fixing a broken light switch or patching a cracked windowpane. In the country, teen boys lug armfuls of wood indoors for the stove. They help their parents turn soil on their dacha plots and plant and harvest vegetables. They pick their younger siblings up from day care and might assist in watching them until their parents are free.

Teens in Chechnya participating in a home economics class learn to make meals.

25

Religion

Of those Russians who are religious, 15 percent to 20 percent are Russian Orthodox. This faith is the largest Eastern Orthodox church in the world.

Russian Orthodox churches are quite elegant, with colorful domes and intricate artwork. Lights flicker across walls, but these lights aren't of the electrical variety. Most Russian Orthodox churches favor the soft glow of candles that each member lights before the service. Worshippers remain standing during the service out of respect for God's presence. The ceilings are high and domed. Each dome is tipped and

The interior of the dome in St. Petersburg's St. Isaac's Cathedral was painted by Karl Bryullov and is titled Virgin in Glory.

swirled with colors: blue, black, red, and gold. From a distance, these golden, spiraling towers glow like candles.

The ceremonies that take place here are reverent and solemn, and each member must come properly dressed in clean, neat clothing. Women often cover their heads with scarves or shawls and wear skirts.

Large murals and paintings shine down on worshippers from the ceilings and domes. Many churches have extensive collections of holy artifacts. There are large walls of golden statues depicting the lives of the saints. Some churches are home to bodies of saints. These bodies have remained preserved for hundreds of years and attract visitors from around the world.

After the collapse of the Soviet Union in 1991, religious activity in Russia increased sharply. No longer was religion considered to be a person's weakness. People returned to formal houses of worship. But the Orthodox religion is far from the only one practiced in Russia. Muslims make up 10 percent to 15 percent of worshippers in Russia. Other Christian religions are also gaining in popularity. Protestant groups have had communities in Russia since the 17th century and are now estimated to have as many as 5 million members. Roman Catholicism,

Type of Religion	Places of Worship
Russian Orthodox Church	5,000
Muslim	3,000
Baptist	450
Old Believers	more than 200
Roman Catholics	200
Evangelicals	120
Seventh Day Adventists	120
Buddhists	80
Krishanites	68
Jews	50
Unified Evangelical Lutherans	39

Source: Embassy of the Russian Federation.

Moscow's St. Basil's Cathedral was built between 1555 and 1561, and was commissioned by Ivan the Terrible.

Judaism, and Buddhism all have stable followings.

Food and Drink

Traditionally, Russian hosts and hostesses like to see their guests fed properly. They take great pride in building a beautiful meal that stretches from one end of the table to the other. If a Russian family is expecting guests, teen girls will spend a long day in the kitchen with their mothers, preparing dozens of trays of hors d'oeuvres.

The Russian diet is one of predictability—meals have recurring staples and favorites. Foods such as potatoes, red beets, and soup are quite accurately associated with Russian cuisine. Tea is also a staple in the diets of Russians.

Tea might be consumed with a sandwich for breakfast, or it might be enjoyed as an after-dinner drink. But most importantly, Russians enjoy drinking tea in the company of friends. Some may add a slice of lemon to their tea, and drink it with chocolate, cookies, candy, cake, preserves, or honey. Tea imported from India is the most popular in Russia but many Russians like drinking herbal teas as well, such as mint or

Russians usually prefer tea to coffee, and they tend to drink it after eating a meal.

Russians enjoy drinking tea with chocolates.

black currant varieties, and they often grow these in their own gardens.

Soup is also popular, and *borsch*, or beet soup, is a favorite. When it's done cooking, the soup glows an intense red from the beets, and hearty chunks of meat, cabbage, and potatoes bob to the surface. Russians often add a dollop of sour cream and a sprinkling of parsley or fresh dill to the soup right before spooning the first bites into their mouths.

Pirozhki are a hit at parties. Teens will snatch at trays piled high with these delicate, homemade pies. The fillings can range from the savory—chopped cabbage, ground meat, or sliced mushrooms—to the sweet—sugared

borsch
BORSCH

pirozhki
peeh-rash-KEEH

Fast Food, Russian Style

The American chain McDonald's is very popular in Russia, and the restaurants can be found sprouting up on many city corners. Not to be outdone by this fast-food phenomenon, Russian businessmen invented chains of small restaurants that serve local-style fast food. At Kroshka-Kartoshka, potatoes are baked and stuffed with cheese and vegetables. Another Russian fast-food haven, Russkoe Bistro, serves items such as stuffed rolls with meat or vegetable fillings to more than 400 hungry people per day!

There are about 150 McDonald's restaurants throughout Russia. The busiest McDonald's in the world is located in Pushkin Square in Moscow. It's workers serve close to 30,000 people per day.

apricots or other fruits.

Families who live in the Russian countryside make use of their surroundings. They hunt through prickly berry patches in the forest to find and harvest wild cranberries, blueberries, strawberries, raspberries, and blackberries. After they are gathered, the women boil, strain, and mash them to make jams, desserts, preserves, and drinks.

Health

It is the goal to make health care available to all Russian citizens. About 4 percent of the salary of a working Russian is taken out of each paycheck, and this money is designated to cover basic health care. The government is required to make its own contributions to the country's medical insurance fund, which would cover any nonemployed citizens such as children, retired

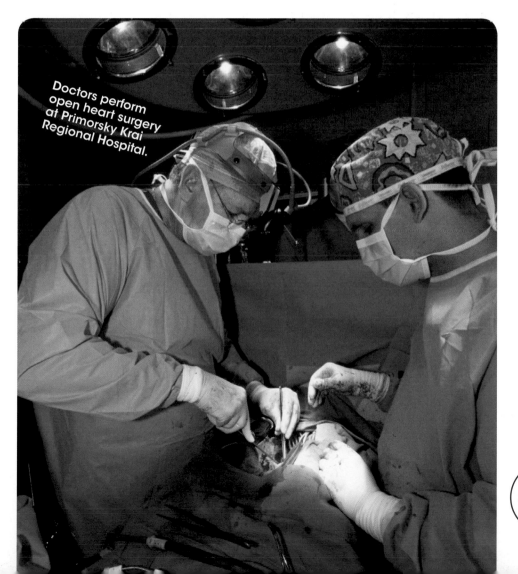

Doctors perform open heart surgery at Primorsky Krai Regional Hospital.

adults, and the mentally and physically disabled. While this should guarantee that Russian teens have access to ample medical assistance and therefore be of good health, this is not the case.

Some hospitals are in desperate conditions. There is improper sanitation and a shortage of beds and staff. Parents sometimes have to act as informal nurses—washing, preparing meals, and cleaning—when their children go into the hospital, because the nurses are too busy and overextended to give full and proper care. Doctors are undertrained and underpaid—making an average of 1,350 rubles (U.S.$50) per month. There is only one doctor for every 275 Russian citizens. Families living in rural areas find it almost impossible to obtain decent care. Families in urban areas have better access to health care professionals and clinics, but might still find it difficult to get the correct and most affordable medicine.

Hospitals and doctors might be

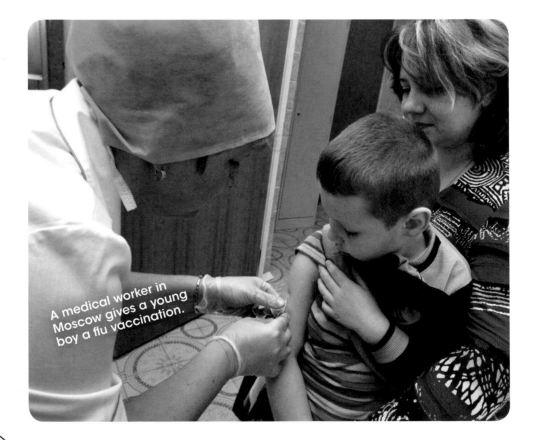

A medical worker in Moscow gives a young boy a flu vaccination.

hard to find, but this isn't the only problem with Russia's overall health situation. Poor diet and lack of proper exercise also contributes to the declining well-being of the nation's citizens. Growing seasons are short, so fruits and vegetables are difficult to grow, and the variety found in grocery stores is often too expensive. Air and water are sometimes clogged with toxins caused by runoff from factories and agricultural sites. In fact, one in five water taps in Russia is contaminated to the point of not being drinkable.

Because of these and other health hazards such as stress, tobacco and drug use, and alcohol abuse, life expectancy is low. Males have an average life expectancy of 59 years. Females have a better outlook—their average life expectancy is now 72 years.

Russian women worry about their health and the health of their unborn children. According to the deputy health minister, 80 percent of expectant mothers have some sort of complication during pregnancy. In 2002, the Russian Ministry of Health declared that about two-thirds of Russian infants were born unhealthy, and about half of Russia's expectant mothers were malnourished. Birthrates are falling each year because, with worsening living conditions and the health situation for pregnant women, many young couples are postponing their decision to have children or are deciding to have just one child. In 2006, the average number of children

per family was about one.

Alcoholism is another health issue plaguing the country. The country's

To help improve Russia's health situation, UNICEF is working with the Russian government and has established the Youth-Friendly medical and social services program in nine regions of Russia. This program helps teach young people about their own reproductive health.

Chemical Pollution in Russia

The pollution of Russia's rivers is a big factor in the health of the nation. Illegal chemical dumping and other unsafe practices have severely contaminated the water. Disease-causing bacteria are found in the Moscow River on a regular basis. Russians have been urged to boil their water before using it—just to be safe.

Chemicals such as heavy metals and pesticides have been dumped into the Volga River in large quantities.

Of course, the Volga isn't the only contaminated body of water. The Arctic Ocean, north of Russia, has also had its share of pollution. In the 1960s, dozens of nuclear reactors were taken apart and dumped into this ocean. This illegal dumping has had far-reaching effects on the health of many Russian citizens.

Even worse than chemical dumping was the disastrous explosion of the nuclear power plant in Chernobyl in 1986. The blast sent radioactive debris into the sky. The waste floated over western Russia, causing 200,000 people to be evacuated. It's hard to assess the damage that the accident caused. Deaths at the time were numerous and the instances of cancer are projected to be astronomical. About 4,000 deaths could ultimately be attributed to the Chernobyl accident.

drinking age is 21, but it is not always followed. Alcohol use by women, men, and even teens is skyrocketing. Vodka is the nation's official and most popular drink. It's often the main focus of social interactions. Russians believe you should never drink alone, so people often enjoy vodka together.

The Russian people are known to be excellent hosts and can usually find something to toast. But often there is no such thing as a single toast. In fact, toasts can be long-winded and detailed. The first round of toasting is in honor of the reason for the gathering. It can even be as simple as toasting to friendship. The next round is dedicated to the host of the get-together. The third is reserved for love. And after three toasts, it is easy to slip into even more.

The alcohol consumption that takes place at traditional social functions can become a habit and then, eventually, an addiction. Even Russian teens need to be concerned about the alcoholism crisis in Russia. Out of 100,000 teens, it is estimated that 18 of them are alcoholics. The problem is now receiving much attention from the media and the government. Steps are being taken in Russia and abroad to develop campaigns to help stop excessive drinking.

A Russian family living in St. Petersburg toasts during dinner.

Music clubs are popular places for teens to hang out with their friends.

3

Fast Friends, Forever Family

"BORYA! GRISHA! MILA! DASHA!" Teens rush toward the doors of the school. They call to their friends. "Lika! Petya! Vadik!" Crowding around in groups, they talk excitedly about the weekend. What is there to do? Movies? Ballet? Ice skating? A concert? The sounds of students making plans buzzes through the halls.

This is a common scene after a long day of school. Russian teens can make friends fast and keep them close. If teens can't see their friends at school, they can call or sometimes e-mail them to find out what's going on.

37

What's In a Name?
Popular Russian Names
and Nicknames

Male Names

Name	Nickname
Aleksei	Alyosha
Anton	Antosha
Dmitriy	Dima
Grigoriy	Grisha
Ivan	Vanya
Mikhail	Misha
Sergei	Seryozha
Stanislav	Stas
Viktor	Vitya
Vladimir	Vova
Yuriy	Yura

Female Names

Name	Nickname
Anastasia	Nastya
Anna	Anya
Dariya	Dasha
Galina	Galya
Irina	Ira
Kseniya	Ksyusha
Natalya	Natasha
Oksana	
Svetlana	Sveta
Tatiyana	Tanya
Yekaterina	Katya

There are 74 million cell phones in use across Russia. They are popular with teens who like to have the newest and most technologically advanced models to show off at school. Russian teens who have cell phones can use them to send text messages to their friends, ask about homework, or organize a trip to a dance club.

Internet service is expensive but growing, and teens in larger cities now have regular access to chat rooms, message boards, and popular e-mail services. Approximately 23.7 million Russians are Internet users.

Family

Times can be hard in a country that is still trying to find its footing after an era of unstable, damaging government. The job market is weak. Pay is low. Houses are crumbling. The future looks bleak. This is how it has been for Russians since the Soviet reign ended in 1991, and

Although Russian citizens enjoy new technology, they have also placed importance on preserving the past in buildings such as St. Basil's Cathedral.

SAMSUNG

E720

some of those problems continue today. However, families can provide stability in the face of all of these daunting changes.

It's easy to see why close family ties provide a source of strength and support. Life—especially for teens who are going through so many changes—can be difficult. Even though the family unit is sacred to many Russians, families are getting smaller.

39

Russian families are shrinking in size, and the government is concerned about it. Recently, one government official suggested imposing a tax upon families who choose not to have any children.

Teens are important building blocks of the family. They are entrusted with the care of their younger siblings, and they often help in their spoiling! Taking them on walks, chasing them around playgrounds, teaching them how to skate or sled—these are all things teens do to help their parents with child care. Along with babysitting, teens also help their parents with duties around the house. They help keep things in order and make sure the daily routines run smoothly. Often, the whole family works together to make sure that each day goes well.

A Woman's Work

Russian women make lists and run to the grocery store for the week's food. But because a majority of Russian families—about 70 percent—don't own cars, the groceries are carried home in their arms. They prepare all the family's meals. They scour pots, pans, and plates after everyone is finished. They hang the washed clothes out to dry and then wrap them in tiny bundles. The women of Russia are the ones who are responsible for many of the household chores. Little girls, teens, and adult women usually share equally in the division of household labor.

If Russian teen girls choose to enter the job market as adults, they will have excellent benefits if they decide to also have children. Russian law allows for fully paid maternity leave for 70 days prior to and after giving birth. Some companies also provide free or affordable day care services right at the office.

A woman in Yekaterinburg carries her groceries.

Teens in Moscow celebrate Novyi God, or New Year's Day, by lighting firecrackers.

4

A Full Year of Festivities

THE SHOPKEEPERS TURN OFF THEIR LIGHTS and bolt the doors. The streets empty. Suddenly, there is laughter and cheering everywhere. Someone is singing. The tiny houses and apartments that line the streets glow. Inside them, rooms are crowded with people. Tables sag under the weight of trays of steaming food—thick twists of bread or mounds of sweet pastries.

When Russians celebrate, they make sure to do it right! Family and friends set aside their work, studies, and worries to observes together. Russians are very serious about their celebrations and have hundreds of festivals, holidays, and joyful traditions on their yearly calendar. In fact, they could spend the whole year in one gigantic party if everybody celebrated all the special days.

43

National Holidays

Novyi God (New Year's Day)—January 1

Rozhdestvo (Christmas)—January 7

Tatiana's Day (Student's Day)—January 25

St. Valentine's Day—February 14

Den' Zashchitnika Otechestva (Defender of the Fatherland Day)—February 23

Maslenitsa (Pancake Day)—on the Sunday 40 days prior to Russian Orthodox Easter

International Women's Day—March 8

Paskha (Orthodox Easter)—date determined by calculations based on the Julian calendar

The Holiday of Spring and Labor—May 1

Victory Day—May 9

Russia Day—June 12

The Day of Knowledge—September 1

The International Day of Peace—September 1

yolkas
YOHL-kahs

Novyi God

The celebratory calendar starts out with Novyi God, or New Year's Day. New Year's is one of the most important days of the entire year for the Russian people. Teens help their parents decorate *yolkas* (fir trees) and small children wait for the mythical Grandfather Frost to journey down from his home in Velikiy Ustug to deliver presents. This town is at the very top of Russia, and it would be a difficult trip to make if Grandfather Frost didn't have some help. Therefore, his beautiful Snow Maiden granddaughter always helps him hand out his presents while bells ring out across the country.

At midnight, the president appears on television to give a special toast for the new year. After his speech is done, adults join in champagne toasts with their families and eat a late meal before heading outside. They join other families in dancing, watching fireworks, and more feasting.

Grandfather Frost and the Snow Maiden are symbols of the Russian celebration of Novyi God.

Rozhdestvo

Another major January holiday—Rozhdestvo, or Christmas—is on January 7th. While New Year's is considered the most festive holiday in Russia, many teens celebrate Rozhdestvo just as heartily. As part of tradition, a fast is held on Christmas Eve day. The end of the fast is marked by a solemn evening church service. After church, Russian teens scramble to get home, where they devour large helpings of a special type of porridge called *kutya*—a rich, sweet

kutya
kooh-TYAH

45

A group of young Russian women dress in traditional clothing to celebrate Rozhdestvo.

food studded with walnuts, apricots, raisins, and poppy seeds.

After the meal, gifts are distributed, and teens follow their parents in prayers for a good year as well as for the strength to live better and purer lives.

Den' Zashchitnika Otechestva

Den' Zashchitnika Otechestva—Defender of the Fatherland Day—falls on February 23. Originally a day reserved to honor the history of Russian soldiers and the military, this day has become more of a national men's day. Russian men felt left out after years of celebrating International Women's Day, which falls in March. This day now allows men to have a little attention of their own. Women spend the day showering their men with congratulations, gifts, and words of praise and love. A man's wife might make his favorite meal as a sign of appreciation. Russian teens might lavish their fathers with hugs,

A war veteran stands at attention at a demonstration in Stavropol on Den' Zashchitnika Otechestva.

kisses, or back rubs to make him feel relaxed on his special day.

Maslenitsa

February rounds out with the celebration of Maslenitsa, which is sometimes called Pancake Day. Russian teens wave goodbye to winter with this celebration. They enjoy the warming temperatures and the promise of spring. They chase each other through the melting snowbanks and beg for rides on *troikas*, or sleighs. Later teen girls will join their mothers in the kitchen and churn out towering stacks of warm *bliny,* or

troikas
TROY-kahs

bliny
bleeh-NEEH

St. Valentines Day

February's holiday of St. Valentine's Day has recently become popular in Russia. It is celebrated with candies, cakes, and other sweets. Russian teens might exchange small gifts or cards as tokens of affection for their boyfriends or girlfriends.

47

Maslenitsa is sometimes celebrated with the burning of a straw figure as a way of saying goodbye to winter.

pancakes. After this comforting meal, it's back outside. They know this might be one of their last chances to play in the winter weather for a whole year.

Throughout Russia, people celebrate with music, entertainment, food, games, and prizes for families and kids. Sometimes, costumed actors run around warding off evil spirits.

International Women's Day

The month of March begins with International Women's Day. This is a day when all Russian females can expect to receive compliments.

This special day for women is celebrated in other countries as well, but Russians started celebrating it during the Soviet period as a way to show that women had equality in the country. While it may have lost some of its social significance since the end of Soviet rule, International Women's Day still celebrates the strength, love, power, and beauty of Russian women.

Paskha

Paskha, or Easter, is another very important holiday in Russia. It is always celebrated on the first Sunday after the vernal equinox. This celebration is especially important to Russians who are part of the Russian Orthodox Church. They spend the day reflecting on the life of Jesus and his resurrection.

Orthodox Russians spend their Easters fasting. The fast is broken after a church service during which baskets full of Easter eggs—colored red, often by boiling them with onion skins—are blessed by the priest. Returning home,

In a village near Lake Baikal, women walk home arm in arm celebrating International Women's Day.

teens feast on a simple meal of eggs, bread, and a rich dessert called *kulich*, which is a yeasty bread flavored with lemon, almonds, and raisins. Kulich is a very special tradition in Russia. After being baked in a tall cylinder, the kulich is taken from the oven and covered with white frosting. Sometimes, on one side of the cake, the Cyrillic letters "XB" are spelled out with candies. "XB" stands for "Christ is risen," reminding the Russian people of Christ's resurrection.

Easter is also a time for families to visit the graves of their departed relatives.

kulich
kooh-LICH

On Paskha, celebrations often feature kulich and eggs.

Fabergé Eggs

The most famous Easter eggs of all time are the Fabergé eggs made by St. Petersburg jeweler Peter Carl Fabergé. In 1884, Tsar Alexander III asked Fabergé to make a very special Easter present for his wife, the tsarina Maria. Eggs reminded her of her homeland of Denmark, so Fabergé set out to create the most beautiful egg ever seen. The tsarina was overjoyed at her present, and the tsar commissioned an egg to be created every year.

Fabergé used a variety of metals and ornate jewels such as sapphires, rubies, emeralds, and diamonds to decorate the eggs. The designs were kept as surprises until they were revealed on Easter. They often displayed scenes or portraits. Some of the famed Fabergé eggs showed scenes of the Trans-Siberian Railroad, the crowning of new tsars, anniversaries, and even the work of the Red Cross during wartime.

All over the world, the Fabergé eggs are admired for their beauty, painstaking detail, and creativity. Today, 50 of the eggs are on display in museums across the world, in places such as New York City, Moscow, London, and Monaco.

They pay their respects and leave small tokens of appreciation—small toys or flowers—and food for those who have passed on.

Russia Day

June starts out with a bang when Russians celebrate their Independence Day on the 12th. This occasion, also called Russia Day, is the newest of the Russian holidays. In 1991, the Declaration of Russian Sovereignty was adopted after the breakup of the Soviet Union. It's a day for Russians to rejoice

The History of the Russian Flag

The Russian flag is made up of three horizontal stripes of white, blue, and red. It was originally designed in the 1600s after Peter the Great, one of Russia's most influential rulers, traveled to the Netherlands to learn about shipbuilding. He was so impressed with that country's flag—with its three horizontal bands of red, white, and blue—that he patterned his own after it and had it designed for his fleet of ships.

The top white layer stands for sincerity. The middle blue layer represents truthfulness. The bottom layer of red signifies bravery and love.

The flag design was abandoned during the Soviet period in favor of a solid red flag decorated with a hammer, sickle, and star. The hammer symbolized the nation's industrial workers. The sickle represented agricultural citizens. Finally, the five-pointed star rising above the hammer and sickle represented the rule of the Communist Party.

After the fall of communism in August 1991, the old design was restored.

Teens sing the national anthem during a concert in Moscow celebrating Russia Day.

and remember their country's history. They think back on the first shaky years of independence and hope for continued improvements and strength for the future of their country. Elaborate parades are held in Moscow, and Russia's colors are unfurled in celebration.

Weddings, Births, and Funerals

Each and every day, the Russian people gather with family and close friends to observe and celebrate weddings, births, and deaths. These traditions might be less public in nature, but they are no less elaborate than holiday celebrations.

And elaborate is the right word to describe a Russian wedding ceremony. They are so detailed that the celebrations may continue for two days.

Weddings begin at the house where the bride lives. The groom and his friends arrive in a caravan of cars. When they try to get to the bride, they might have to pay a small fee to the bride's friends or perform complex tasks before they can even be in the same room with her. A groom might have to go through a test to see if he can select

53

Newlyweds celebrate their wedding day on an embankment of the Neva River in St. Petersburg.

his bride's lipstick marks in a pile of napkins imprinted with kisses.

After finally getting in to see his bride, the groom gathers the families and leads them in a procession to the local registry office where all weddings take place. Many Russian couples have symbolic church weddings as well.

The actual wedding ceremony is standard and quick. After the newlyweds sign official documents, exchange wedding rings, and kiss, the real celebration begins. It is tradition that the bride and groom be driven around to important sites of local history. They make stops at monuments and the eternal flame that

Newlyweds in St. Petersburg release two white doves to symbolize their new life together.

The Wedding Cars

Russian weddings aren't hard to identify. If you happened to be walking down a street and suddenly saw a line of decorated cars, you'd know where they were headed. The Russian people aren't shy about showing off for weddings. Cars are often adorned with colorful balloons, ribbons, and flowers.

commemorates Russians who were lost in World War II. There they lay flowers out of respect and in remembrance. After these stops, the wedding party heads to the reception for a party that could last up to two days.

Practical jokes are traditionally a large part of the wedding reception. The bride and groom are made to overcome many obstacles during their party. They might have to sweep up coins thrown to the floor by prankster guests or take bites of a piece of bread to decide who will become the head of the household. The person with the bigger bite wins.

Birthdays are also joyous occasions for Russian teens. The days are filled with presents, special foods, and family parties. Mothers often spend extra time in the kitchen, preparing special birthday feasts and cakes. After family parties, teens may have another celebration with their friends and go out dancing or see a movie. In a similar way, Russian teens celebrate the day of the saint they are named after. On these days, called *imeniny*, small presents and special meals are prepared to honor the occasion.

When there is a death in a family, it is handled in a very private manner. The family of the deceased will mourn

A young woman celebrates her birthday with her husband.

A Russian family holds a memorial service at the Apostle Andrew Church in Moscow.

and mark their mourning by covering mirrors in the house for a period after the death. Traditionally, Russians believe that mirrors are very powerful objects. They cover them after deaths to avoid seeing the dead spirit still floating in the house. Covering the mirrors also helps the spirits escape. It is believed the spirits can be snared by the mirror and be held earthbound. Covered mirrors are said to set the spirits free.

imeniny
eeh-meeh-NEEH-neeh

A series of gatherings for family members begins on the day of the burial. At least two more gatherings may follow according to Russian Orthodox religious beliefs: one on the ninth day after the person died, and another marking the one-year anniversary of the loved one's death. At these gatherings, people remember the deceased and share a meal.

Teens often find work in the services industry, which makes up 68.3 percent of all jobs in the country.

5 Teens at Work

LIKE TEENS ALL OVER THE WORLD, Russian teens can have typical first jobs. Girls might babysit, wait tables, answer phones at a small business, or work at fast-food restaurants. Boys might wash dishes at a café, sell food as street vendors, or offer their services as handymen.

After secondary school, many teens will go on to college. Some will go to vocational school. Still others will become part of the Novye Russkie, an elite class of wealthy Russians. These teens will graduate from college and head for well-paying jobs in the big cities. They will hustle down the street toward the glittering buildings of Moscow and St. Petersburg, their expensive shoes hitting the pavement with authority. They will give orders on their cell phones and breeze into conference rooms. Teens who successfully achieve this status will be part of the fast-paced, post-Soviet economy. They might spend their days as bankers and stockbrokers. They might be in charge of the investment and trading worlds of Russia's new economy, and they could be very wealthy. With that in mind, they head off for these jobs in herds, hoping to have even half the success of the flashy

Labor force by occupation

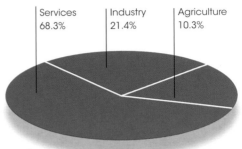

| Services 68.3% | Industry 21.4% | Agriculture 10.3% |

Source: United States Central Intelligence Agency.

The Russian Mafiya

In Russia, the concept of mafiya, or mafia, isn't just something people see on television or at the movies. It's a real problem. Each day, more and more Russian teens—mostly boys, but sometimes girls—are seduced into this gang lifestyle.

The Russian mafiya is a large network of gangsters, dishonest businessmen, and corrupt government officials who will take bribes in exchange for favors. Unlike Western mafias, Russia's does not deal mostly in drug trafficking or prostitution. It is a more complex, complicated business

that controls many corporations. Members skim money off the tops of these corporations' profits every day.

It's no surprise, then, that members of the mafiya are rich, flashy, and elegant. They career around town in expensive cars. They are able to dine at the best restaurants. They are seen with the most beautiful women. Russian teens are impressed, and many of them want the same things. Each year, more and more teens go off to join the ranks of the mafiya, becoming part of the country's large and complex crime family.

A combine harvests wheat in a field in the Chelyabinsk region.

and well-groomed people they see on the streets.

Teens who live in the country are part of families that often make their living in agriculture. Life in rural Russia follows a very precise routine devoted to the production of crops—such as wheat, flax, sugar beets, and potatoes—and the caring of livestock. Some teens will follow in their parents' footsteps and stay on the family land to tend to the farms. For the most part, though, few Russian teens want to stay in the countryside. They are lured toward the cities

61

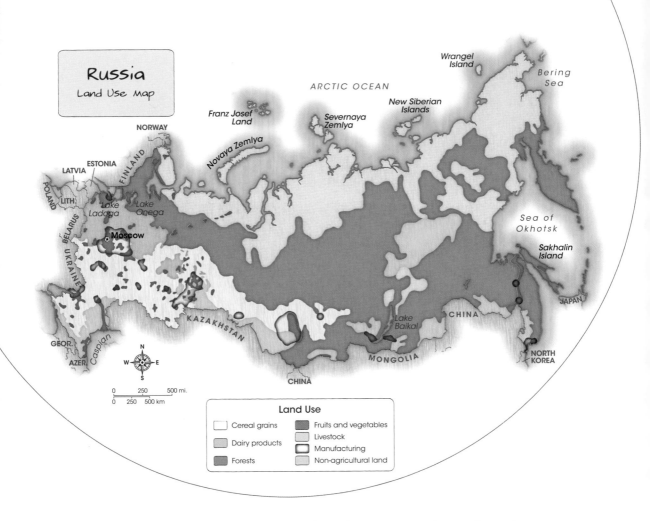

Russia
Land Use Map

ARCTIC OCEAN

Wrangel
Island

Bering
Sea

Franz Josef
Land

New Siberian
Islands

NORWAY

Severnaya
Zemlya

Novaya Zemlya

ESTONIA
LATVIA
FINLAND

POLAND
LITH.

Lake
Ladoga

Lake
Onega

Sea of
Okhotsk

BELARUS

Moscow

Sakhalin
Island

UKRAINE

KAZAKHSTAN

Lake
Baikal

CHINA

JAPAN

GEOR.

Caspian

AZER.

N
W — E
S

CHINA

MONGOLIA

NORTH
KOREA

0   250   500 mi.
0   250   500 km

Land Use

Cereal grains

Fruits and vegetables

Dairy products

Livestock

Manufacturing

Forests

Non-agricultural land

by the exciting stories they hear and the glamorous lives they see on television.

Serving Their Country

Russian teen boys are involuntarily registered for the draft at the age of 17. If they voluntarily enter military service after secondary school, they can select which branch interests them the most. Teen girls interested in the military may join as well. The Russian military has a large reserve of ground, naval, air, air defense, and strategic rocket forces. After entering at the age of 18, teens will serve two years before being discharged.

Upset about the lies and actions of their government during the Soviet years, some of Russia's youth are not interested in joining the military. A recent poll showed 50 percent of Russians support an all-volunteer force.

Russian recruits make their way to the military units in which they will serve.

Hazing is also a concern for those who want to join the military. Dmitriy Andriyanov, who lives in Penza, says he looked forward to joining the army at the age of 18, but that all changed after he watched a documentary on the Russian army.

"I saw a TV episode about one young soldier who was beaten so bad that they had to amputate his legs," Dmitriy says. The documentary changed his mind, and now he is uncertain if he wants to enter the military.

Women in the Workplace

Russian girls go further in the educational system than boys do. Despite this, they are consistently kept out of upper management positions. On average, women earn significantly less than men who have the exact same jobs and experience as they do.

A female receptionist works at the Hotel Kempiniski in Moscow.

Even though the expanding economy is opening new job opportunities for teens, old stereotypes remain. The most common job for a young woman is that of secretary. Advertisements searching for candidates often list physical attractiveness as a requirement.

Professional Salaries

Salaries in Russia are often not in line with the prices of necessities. For instance, doctors in Russia are also severely underpaid. The average monthly salary for Russian doctors who work in smaller cities is 5,000 rubles

(U.S.$186), but in Moscow, the average salary for doctors is 25,000 rubles (U.S.$930) per month. This striking difference in salaries is also apparent in other professions.

Teachers in smaller cities earn an average monthly salary of 4,812 rubles (U.S.$179), but in Moscow their salaries average 8,000 rubles (U.S.$298) per month. The salaries in the smaller cities can become a burden when one considers the price of some common necessities. For instance, it isn't uncommon to spend 1,500 rubles (U.S.$56) on a pair of shoes, or 2,000 rubles (U.S.$74) on a pair of winter boots. Those prices are more than 30 percent of the average teacher's monthly salary! This unbalanced equation makes it difficult for some Russians to afford clothing, transportation, entertainment, and other daily items.

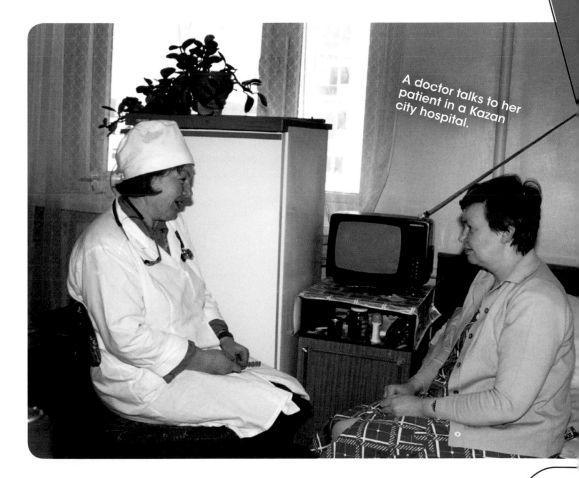

A doctor talks to her patient in a Kazan city hospital.

A teenager watches a performance during Live 8 Moscow at Red Square. The free concert helps raise awareness for an organization called Make Poverty History.

6

Russia is Never Boring!

DURING GLASNOST, the teen culture of Russia revolutionized. Some teens were tired of the censorship and lies that filled their lives during the 1980s. They were distrustful of those who had allowed the nation to slip so easily into disrepair. More than anything, teens wanted to separate themselves from the older generations. They wanted to show everyone they were different. Disillusioned with government, corporations, and adults, teens started to demand more independence and control. Currently teens have more freedom than ever before. These freedoms are frequently expressed through the movies they watch, the music they listen to, and the other choices they make in ways to fill up their free time.

The Cinema Experience

Movies from the West—especially Hollywood—are popular choices among Russian teens. Hundreds of movie theaters fill with teens excited to see popular American movies in which the conversations are often dubbed in Russian. Generally, Russian teens see more movies from Hollywood than from their own country. The Russian movie business has been struggling since 1991.

During the Soviets' reign, movies were censored. Producers, directors, and actors had to be careful if they were dealing with taboo subject matter. The Soviets did not want to advocate sex or violence in movies. They wanted movies to be uplifting and pro-Soviet Union. Teens tended to stay away from propaganda movies during this time. They wanted to stare up at the giant screen and watch movies with action, love, adventure, comedy, or splashy visual effects.

After the Soviet Union's collapse, restrictions on movies were lifted. This meant that movies were able to be more explicit and would reach a wider audience. Documentaries that exposed lies and atrocities committed by the Soviet government became commonplace. Moviegoing teens flooded the theaters to try to understand parts of their country's history—parts that had been hidden from them by the Soviet government. These movies helped teens define their country and—better yet—themselves.

Of course, the end of censorship also had some negative results. Suddenly, psychotic madmen, rib-shattering violence, and never-before-seen portrayals of sex were splashing across the screen. Teens may have been excited by this new graphic cinema experience, but their parents were not.

A teenager looks at DVD movies that are on display at a stall in a Moscow subway station.

Movie attendance started falling in the 1990s because of the new type of cinema and skyrocketing prices. This trend has started to reverse, however, and Russians are again seeking a form of escape from their daily lives at the movie theater.

There are several types of movie theaters in Russia. Some are housed in older buildings with only one screen. A ticket to see a movie at these theaters costs about 27 rubles (U.S.$1).

Russia's Big Trilogy

Hollywood loves a good trilogy. Blockbusters packaged in threes prove popular with production companies, theaters, and viewing audiences around the world. Movies like *Back to the Future, Lord of the Rings,* and both the original and new versions of *Star Wars* were packaged in threes and eaten up at the box office.

Not to be outdone, Russia's movie business is now realizing the potential for their own trilogies. Released in 2004, *Night Watch* sold more tickets and beat out all the Western films at the Russian box office—a rare accomplishment. Its follow-up, *Day Watch,* shattered all box-office records to become the most successful Russian movie of all time. The third installment has a 2007 debut.

This new supernatural trilogy is set in modern-day Russia. The characters have superhuman powers and must choose to fight for either the side of Light or the side of Dark. With body snatching, fast cars, and mystical tools like an all-powerful chalk that can rewrite people's fate, Russian audiences were stunned by the never-before-seen special effects and the intricate plot line. The movies are based on a science-fiction trilogy by popular author Sergei Lukyanenko. *Night Watch* has grossed more than 695,500,000 rubles (U.S.$26 million), which is a staggering figure. Normally, it is unusual if a Russian movie passes the 53,500,000 ruble (U.S.$2 million) mark.

69

Newer theaters can house more than one screen—although multiplexes have been generally unsuccessful across the country—and they also provide other entertainment opportunities, such as arcade games. A ticket at the newer theaters cost around 216 rubles (U.S.$8).

Upscale concessions are becoming more popular in movie theaters. While snacks like popcorn and soda are served, newer theaters are bringing in small cafés that provide alcoholic beverages, coffees, and full meals.

Music and Nightlife

To get away from everyday stresses, teens in Russia's biggest cities like Moscow and St. Petersburg formed elaborate musical undergrounds. Music lovers who had been listening to bootlegged copies of Western music began to produce and distribute music that had been previously censored or forbidden. Recordings of Western rock 'n' roll and Russian folk music were tucked into pockets, purses, and backpacks and then passed from teen to teen.

Teens attend a rock concert at the Bunker, a night club in Moscow.

Magnitizdat

Soviet rule led to many different types of censorship. Books, movies, and music all received increasing amounts of pressure to be "clean" and "uplifting." In this environment, there was no room for criticism or social protest in entertainment. But this didn't stop some Russians—especially enterprising teenagers! When they couldn't go to a record store to buy the Western music they were interested in—music that had been deemed corruptive and scandalous by the Soviets—they took matters into their own hands.

Magnitizdat—Russia's musical underground—helped circulate illegal recordings of many types of banned music. Russian teens and music lovers would purchase X-ray plates for a very low price and then record music onto them. Tape recorders were also used to mass-produce copies of this music.

It wasn't just Western rock 'n' roll that was banned from the country at that time. Dance music, Russian folk music, and even Russian rock bands were strictly prohibited. This didn't stop the bands or their fans. Creative teens would organize unofficial and intimate concerts—*kvartirniki*—in apartments so Russian bands could still reach their audience.

kvartirniki
kvahr-TEEHR-neeh-keeh

Russian rock has always been very bass-driven and poetic. Rock artists place just as much emphasis on the words of their songs as they do on the rhythms and sounds that accompany them. Artists often see their songs as forms of social protest. Songs often have to do with the country's politics. Rockers aren't just singing about love; instead, their songs have a much deeper purpose and meaning.

Of course, performing controversial songs hasn't always been an easy task. As late as the 1980s, the work of Russian artists was still being censored. The KGB—the Soviet police agency—seemed concerned about the power of rock 'n' roll. Many feared it would start riots. Because of the threat of prison time, many musicians were forced to lead double lives. They held regular jobs during the day such as plumbers, parking attendants, or salesmen.

The serious rock music of the 1980s and 1990s has been pushed to the side by an emerging popular music scene. Groups like t.A.T.u. rule the charts and even enjoy some crossover success outside of the country. Although shocking to some older Russians, teens were and still are intrigued by t.A.T.u.—a name which, in Russian slang, means "that girl loves that girl."

Much of contemporary Russian music is a clever mix of rock and pop. No band illustrates this more than Mumiy Troll. Originally from the port city of Vladivostok, Mumiy Troll devel-

The Russian duo t.A.T.u. performs on stage.

oped a cult following. Later, the band launched its music into a larger audience, developing what it calls "rocka-pops"—a blend of pop and rock styles influenced by the snappy rhythms of the British music movement of the 1990s, called "Britpop." Mumiy Troll is one of Russia's most popular bands of all time. When Mumiy Troll was new to the music scene, the Soviets labeled them "the most socially dangerous band in Russia." They still proudly carry that label and are viewed as national heartthrobs.

More than just pop and rock crowd the charts in Russia. Agata Kristi is a band that hammers out loud music with a hard and heavy Gothic influence. The super successful band Aquarium, led by Boris Grebenshikov, has remained

The Russian band Mumiy Troll has been recording and performing their music for more than 20 years.

popular for many years. The band has released albums of both straight rock 'n' roll and more traditional Russian folk music. Ivanushki International is a boy band that has Russian girls snatching up their records. DJ Groove, a popular club DJ, keeps Russia's nightclub scene fresh and brimming with the thumping beats of new house music.

All these musical styles mix together on the busy turntables of Russia's nightclubs. While these clubs were at the height of their popularity in the 1980s, they are entering into a revival now. Some clubs host live music showcases that promote local bands. Other clubs blast dance music and teens groove into the early morning hours.

Ballet

Russians believe art belongs to the people—all people. Because of this, many ballet, theater, and opera companies offer tickets to the general public at fairly reasonable prices. If Russian teens are looking for a date idea that won't drain their pockets, they can sometimes find tickets for around 27 rubles (U.S.$1) apiece.

Russians are famous in the world of ballet. This is because Russia's ballet

Zemfira Breaks Boundaries and Records

Like the popular group t.A.T.u., Russian performer Zemfira maintains a large fan base. Her albums deal with issues uncommon in Russian music, such as AIDS and depression. The Russian press has dubbed her "Kurt Cobain in a dress." She has been compared to Elvis, the Sex Pistols, and Courtney Love.

And even though people try to make these comparisons, they still find it difficult to define Zemfira. She is unique, clever, and talented. Most female singers in Russia put out records of predictable and sometimes silly pop songs, but not Zemfira. She has plowed ahead in a traditionally male business and become Russia's Lady of Rock. She writes her own music and arranges it to funky guitar pop. Sometimes she even smoothes some bossa nova and jazz into her music.

Still, no matter what direction she takes, Zemfira's teen fans stay loyal. Thousands of fan sites have sprouted up on the Internet. Message boards flood with fans wanting to trade sighting stories. Fans are always eagerly awaiting her next album's release.

history is long and stunning. Some of the greatest ballet dancers have come from Russia. Anna Pavlova, Natalya Makarova, and Mikhail Baryshnikov stunned 20th century audiences everywhere with their delicate grace and elegant movements. Recent ballet stars include dancers like Anastasia Yatsenko, Andrei Bolotin, and Nelli Kobakhidze of the Bolshoi Ballet company.

Ballet schools across the country are packed with teen hopefuls who

Ballet dancers from Perm, a city in the Urals, perform Serenade at the Bolshoi Theater in Moscow.

want to become the next star. And just as the schools fill with eager students, the theaters fill with a never-ending audience for their talents.

Sports

Russian teens enjoy a variety of sports and keep busy all year round. Soccer, hockey, skateboarding, martial arts, volleyball, and gymnastics—teens have the opportunity to do them all.

Soccer is one of the most popular sports in Russia. The dominant professional league to watch is the Premier-

Teens in Moscow play soccer near Red Square during their school's spring break.

Russian Superstar Athletes

Lyudmila Turishcheva

This four-time Olympic champion in gymnastics was awarded the prestigious Women in Sport trophy by the International Olympic Committee.

Yekaterina Gordeyeva

She and her husband, Sergei Grinkov, twice struck figure skating gold at the Olympics in the pairs competition. Grinkov died unexpectedly of a heart attack before they could defend their title.

Aleksandr Popov

Terrified of the water as a youngster, Popov went on to become one of the best swimmers of all time. He has won numerous Olympic medals in both the 50- and 100-meter races and has been showered with awards including Russian Athlete of the Year and European Sports Press Union Athlete of the Year.

Maria Sharapova

A successful singles tennis player, she enjoyed wins at Wimbledon in 2004 and the U.S. Open in 2006.

Sergei Fedorov

This star forward helped the Russian Olympic hockey teams score a silver medal in the 1998 Winter Olympics and a bronze medal in the 2002 Winter Olympics.

Irina Slutskaya won her seventh European Championship in figure skating in 2006. She has also medaled at two Olympics (a silver in 2002 and a bronze in 2006). Accomplishing this made her one of the most successful figure skaters in the world.

Liga, or Premier League. Of the 16 teams that compete in the league, Lokomotiv Moscow and CSKA Moscow are two of the top teams to watch.

Teens often play in soccer leagues that are part of after-school programs. These programs are usually offered for free, but parents have to purchase the uniforms.

Hockey is also a popular sport in Russia. The Russian Pro Hockey League is the country's professional league. It is composed of two divisions—the Superleague and the Premier League. The Superleague is considered the best league, and is made up of 16 teams.

Vacations

It only takes a train or plane trip for teens to be near a beach. Because Russia's southern coastline skirts the

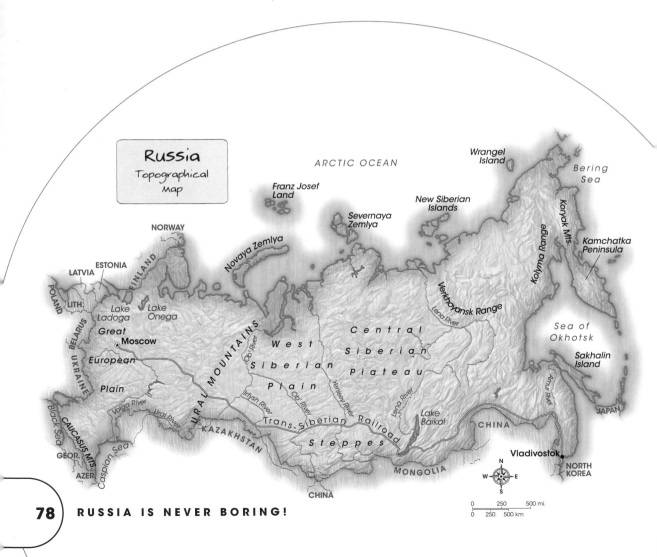

Russia
Topographical
Map

ARCTIC OCEAN

Wrangel Island

Bering Sea

Franz Josef Land

New Siberian Islands

Severnaya Zemlya

Koryak Mts.

Kamchatka Peninsula

NORWAY

Novaya Zemlya

ESTONIA
LATVIA
FINLAND

Verkhoyansk Range

Kolyma Range

POLAND
LITH.
Lake Ladoga
Lake Onega

BELARUS
Great
Moscow

Lena River

Sea of Okhotsk

UKRAINE
European

URAL MOUNTAINS
Ob River

West Siberian Plain

Central Siberian Plateau

Sakhalin Island

Plain

Irtysh River
Ob River
Yenisey River
Lena River

Amur River

Volga River
Ural River
Caspian Sea

Trans-Siberian Railroad

Lake Baikal

CHINA

JAPAN

Black Sea
CAUCASUS MTS.
KAZAKHSTAN

Steppes

GEOR.
AZER.

Vladivostok

MONGOLIA

NORTH KOREA

CHINA

N
W E
S

0   250   500 mi.
0   250 500 km

Russians play beach volleyball near Lake Baikal in Irkutsk.

Black Sea, families living in southern Russia can take inexpensive vacations without leaving the country. Here teens can unwind from school and other pressures by stretching out on the beach or enjoying the resorts that populate the coast.

Another popular vacation spot for Russian families is the picturesque mountainous area surrounding Mineral'nye Vody, the mineral springs near the Caucasus Mountains. Families also enjoy visiting resorts near the Caspian Sea.

Books and Magazines

Everybody has days where they need to stay inside and curl up with a good book. Russian teens are no different. Books,

Popular Contemporary Russian Authors

Aleksandra Marinina

This former employee of the Ministry of the Interior—where she studied Russia's crime world—has been named Writer of the Year and Success of the Year by Russian magazines and festivals.

Viktor Pelevin

He has been hailed as the "great hope of Russian literature." His characters are richly diverse and incredibly complicated.

Boris Akunin

He began his career as a literary critic. He wrote several violent novels set in tsarist Russia, and the public rushed to the bookstore to scoop them up upon release.

the Strugatsky brothers, Boris and the late Arkady. As a rite of passage, some Russian parents pass on well-thumbed copies of the Strugatsky books to their teens. The Strugatsky brothers are still as popular as they were when they first stormed the literary scene in the 1960s.

Contemporary writers are penning fast-paced thrillers. This new literature has much to do with crime and often centers on the Russian mafiya.

Russian literature has a vivid, rich past in the writings of its classical masters. Poet Aleksandr Pushkin is considered one of the fathers of modern Russian literature. Lyev (Leo) Tolstoy is regarded as one of the finest novelists of all times. His most famous works—*War and Peace* and *Anna Karenina*—were widely praised. Fyodor Dostoevsky, another classic novelist, was known for his deep understanding and portrayal of human psychology. Anton Chekhov wrote short stories and plays that are still being produced around the world today.

Joseph Brodsky won a Nobel Prize in 1987 and was chosen to be poet laureate of the United States in 1991. His popularity in Russia was harder to attain. Because he was writing in the late Soviet period, Brodsky produced

like movies, are used as ways to escape from the pressures of everyday life. It's no surprise then that the science-fiction and fantasy genres are so popular among Russian readers.

The most popular sci-fi authors are

work that would have been considered scandalous and therefore censored. To combat the censorship, much of his work was copied—sometimes by hand—and passed on through underground channels. These and other Russian masters still remain quite popular with contemporary teens.

For a more informal reading experience, teens can pick up a copy of any of the most popular Russian magazines. Teens who love gossip can sift through dozens of colorful magazines for their celebrity fix. The magazine *7 Days* is

known for its coverage of today's hottest international superstars. *All Stars*—a similar magazine—reports on the happenings of both Russian and American movie and television stars. The magazine *Girl's Tears* is designed for teen girls, and it reports on all of Russia's latest heartthrobs and popular musical acts.

Many American and British magazines also have counterparts in Russia. Teens have no problem getting their hands on Russian versions of *Cosmopolitan, Marie Claire, Maxim, GQ, and Vogue.*

A statue of the Russian poet Aleksandr Pushkin stands in the city of Pushkin, near St. Petersburg.

АЛЕКСАНДРУ СЕРГѢЕВИЧУ

ПУШКИНУ.

Looking Ahead

THE FUTURE IS PROMISING FOR RUSSIAN TEENS. The relatively new government of the country is working to strengthen its economy and provide its citizens with prosperity. Wages and working conditions are slowly getting better. The residual effects of communism are fading, and now Russia's teens face fewer restrictions than they did under communist rule.

While modern elements of Western culture are crossing Russia's borders in the form of music, fast food, and magazines, Russian teens are still holding fast to old customs. Festivals and holidays feature traditional food, toasts, and superstitions. Russian teens can grab a burger at the local McDonald's or pirozhki from the street vendor whose food is steaming in the open air down the street. And that's the beauty of Russia. It is a country where old meets new, where tradition meets modernization, where rural meets urban, and where all these things mix to create a world of fantastic possibility, where Russian teens can grow up to do or be anything they dream.

At a Glance

Official name: Russian Federation

Capital: Moscow

People

Population: 142,893,540

Population by age group:
0–14 years: 14.2%
15–64 years: 71.3%
65 years and over: 14.4%

Life expectancy at birth: 67.08 years

Official language: Russian

Religion:
Russian Orthodox: 15-20%
Muslim: 10-15%
Other Christian: 2%
Nonpracticing believers or nonbelievers: 73-83%

Legal ages
Alcohol consumption: 21
Driving: 18
Military service: 18
Voting: 18

Government

Type of government: Federation

Chief of state: President, elected by popular vote

Head of government: Premier and Deputy Premier, appointed by the president, with approval from the Duma

Lawmaking body: Federalnoye Sobraniye, or bicameral Federal Assembly, consisting of the Federation Council and the State Duma

Administrative divisions: 49 oblasts, 21 republics, 10 autonomous okrugs, six krays, two federal cities, and one autonomous oblast

Independence: August 24, 1991 (from the Soviet Union)

National symbols: Double-headed eagle, tricolored flag

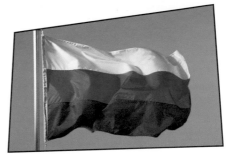

Geography

Total Area: 6,830,080 square miles (17,758,208 square kilometers)

Climate: Ranges from steppes in the south to humid continental in much of Western Russia; subarctic in Siberia to tundra climate in the polar north; winters vary from warm in the steppes to cool along the Arctic coast

Highest point: Gora El'brus, 18,589 feet (5,669 meters)

Lowest point: Caspian Sea, 92.4 feet (28 meters)

Major landforms: Great European Plain, West Siberian Plain, Ural Mountains, Caucasus Mountains

Major rivers and lakes: Amur, Dnieper, Irtysh, Lena, Ob, Volga and Yenisey rivers; Caspian Sea and Lake Baikal, the deepest lake in the world.

Economy

Currency: Russian ruble

Population below poverty line: 17.8%

Major natural resources: Wide natural resource base includes major deposits of oil, natural gas, coal, and many strategic minerals; timber

Major agricultural products: grain, sugar beets, sunflower seed, vegetables, fruits; beef, milk

Major exports: Petroleum and petroleum products, natural gas, wood and wood products, metals, chemicals, and a wide variety of military products

Major imports: Machinery and equipment, consumer goods, medicines, meat, sugar, semifinished metal products

Historical Timeline

The Cold War—
marked by the
strained relationship
between U.S.S.R.
and the United
States—begins

Civil war breaks out in
Russia between the
communist Red Army
and the anticommunist
White Army; millions of
Russians starve during the
communist Red Terror

Napoleon Bonaparte invades
Russia; fire destroys Moscow

🌐 World War I

🌐 World War II

| 1147 | 1689-1725 | 1812 | 1914-1918 | 1917 | 1918-1922 | 1922 | 1939-1945 | 1945 |

Peter the Great
introduces many Western
concepts and creates a
regular army and navy

Russia becomes
part of the newly
formed Union of
Soviet Socialist
Republics (U.S.S.R.)

Moscow first mentioned
in historic chronicles

Bolsheviks rebel against
the Russian government
in the October Revolution

🌐 Historical World Event

President Boris Yeltsin
dissolves Parliament
and has face-off with
conservatives

Soviets place missiles in Cuba,
upsetting the U.S. government
and triggering the tense Cuban
Missile Crisis

Russia becomes
an independent country
as the Soviet Union
collapses

 The first personal
computer in the
world is introduced

| 1950–1953 | 1961 | 1962 | 1969 | 1981 | 1985–1991 | 1989 | 1991 | 1993 |

 The Berlin Wall falls

Soviet cosmonaut
Yuri Gagarin is
the first human to
enter space

General Secretary Mikhail
Gorbachev attempts to
reverse the failing state
of the U.S.S.R.'s economy
with a new policy of
glasnost (openness) and
perestroika (restructuring)

🌐 The Korean War

🌐 Two U.S.
astronauts land
on the moon

Historical Timeline

The Communist Party wins the majority of seats in elections

A school in Beslan is seized by Chechen rebels

After Yeltsin resigns the presidency, Vladimir Putin is elected president

Pluto is demoted to dwarf planet status more than 70 years after its discovery

1994–1996	1995	1998	2000	2001	2002	2004	2006

Work begins on the International Space Station

Huge tsunami strikes nations bordering the Indian Ocean

Russian troops fight war in Chechnya, which has tried to break away from Russia's rule; fighting continues for many years

Terrorist attacks on the two World Trade Center Towers in New York City and on the Pentagon in Washington, D.C., leave thousands dead

Russia and the United States agree on a new reduction of their nuclear arms; skirmishes with Chechen rebels continue

Glossary

bootlegged	produced, distributed, or sold illegally
Cyrillic	alphabet used for writing Russian and other languages of eastern Europe and Asia
glasnost	a Soviet policy permitting open discussion of political and social issues and freer dissemination of news and information
humid continental	type of climate known for its variable weather patterns and temperature ranges; usually found in mid-latitude regions
intricate	highly involved or complex
literacy rate	the percentage of people who are able to read and write
noxious	toxic; hazardous to health
oblasts	a political subdivision of the Russian Federation
okrugs	a political district of the Russian Federation
Old Believers	religious group that separated from the Russian Orthodox Church after reforms took place in 1666 and 1667
perestroika	the policy of economic and governmental reform instituted by Mikhail Gorbachev in the Soviet Union during the mid-1980s
steppe	type of climate in which the soil is too wet to be considered desert, but too dry to support a forest; also has hot summers and cold winters
vernal equinox	the moment when the sun crosses the equator, marking the start of spring in the Northern Hemisphere

Additional Resources

IN THE LIBRARY

Bjornlund, Britta. *The Cold War Ends: 1980 to the Present.* San Diego: Lucent Books, 2003.

Hirschmann, Kristine. *The Deepest Lake.* San Diego: Kidhaven Press, 2003.

Mack, Glenn R., and Asele Surina. *Food Culture in Russia and Central Asia.* Westport, Conn.: Greenwood Press, 2005.

Nardo, Don. *Ivan the Terrible.* Detroit: Blackbirch Press/ Thomas Gale, 2006.

Riordan, James. *Russian Folk-Tales/ Retold by James Riordan.* Oxford, England: Oxford University Press, 2000.

Vail, John J. *Peace, Land, Bread?*: A History of the Russian Revolution. New York: Facts on File, 1996.

ON THE WEB

For more information on this topic, use FactHound.

1. Go to www.facthound.com
2. Type in this book ID: 0756520657
3. Click on the *Fetch It* button.

Look for more Global Connections books.

Teens in Australia

Teens in Brazil

Teens in China

Teens in France

Teens in India

Teens in Israel

Teens in Japan

Teens in Kenya

Teens in Mexico

Teens in Saudi Arabia

Teens in Spain

Teens in Venezuela

Teens in Vietnam

Source Notes

Chapter 2

Page 17, line 22: Nushtayeva, Kristina. Personal interview by Yulia Andriyanova; translated by Svetlana Zhurkin, Compass Point Books. 28 Jan. 2006.

Chapter 5

Page 63, line 8: Andriyanov, Dmitriy. Personal interview by Yulia Andriyanova; translated by Svetlana Zhurkin, Compass Point Books. 29 Jan. 2006.

Select Bibliography

Andriyanov, Dmitriy. Personal Interview by Yulia Andriyanova; translated by Svetlana Zhurkin, Compass Point Books. 29 Jan. 2006.

Astakhova, Eva. "Russia: Film Production and Movie Theaters." Business Information Service for the Newly Independent States. April 2002. 2 Oct. 2006. http://bisnis.doc.gov/bisnis/bisdoc/020429film_ru.htm

CIA World Factbook Online. *Russia*. 2 Nov. 2006. 13 Nov. 2006. www.cia.gov/cia/publications/factbook/geos/rs.html

Embassy of the Russian Federation. *Religion in Russia Today*. Washington, D.C. 25 Oct. 2006. www.russianembassy.org/

The Face of Russia. PBS Online. 2 Oct. 2006. www. pbs.org/weta/faceofrussia/timeline-index.html

Kosarev, Lindsay. "Russian Culture." Suite 101. 2 Oct. 2006. www. suite101.com/lesson.cfm/1808/2211?1=1>

"Light vs. Dark: Russian Vampire Movie Triumphs." Reuters 19 Jan 2005. 20 Dec. 2005, http://movies.yahoo.com/mv/news/va/20060119/113767587600.html

Massey, Stephen. "Russia's Maternal & Child Health Crisis: Socio-Economic Implications and the Path Forward." Johnson's Russia List. 10 Dec. 2002. 30 June 2006. www.cdi.org/russia/johnson/6596-19.cfm

Johnson's Russia List. East West Institute Policy Brief, Vol. 1, No. 9. 11 Dec. 2002. 30 June 2006. www.cdi.org/russia/johnson/6596-19.cfm

"More Than 200 Dead After Troops Storm School." CNN.com. 3 Sept. 2004. Cable News Network. 20 Dec. 2005, www.cnn.com/2004/WORLD/europe/09/03/russia.school/

"Moscow Looks to Helicopter Shuttles to Ease Traffic Problems." *The Word Today*. ABC Local Radio. 23 Feb. 2005. www.abc.net.au/worldtoday/content/2005/s1309365.htm

Nushtayeva, Kristina. Personal Interview by Yulia Andriyanova; translated by Svetlana Zhurkin, Compass Point Books. 28 Jan. 2006.

Shoemaker, Wesley M. *Russia, Eurasian States, and Eastern Europe*. Washington, D.C.: Stryker-Post Publications, 2000.

Vienonen, Mikko A., and Ilkka J. Vohlonen. "Integrated Health Care in Russia: To Be or Not to Be?" International Journal of Integrated Care. 1 March 2001. 2 Oct. 2006. www.ijic.org/publish/issues/2001-1/index.html?000016

Webber, Stephen, and Tatyana Webber. *Teach Yourself Russian Language Life & Culture*. Chicago: McGraw-Hill, 2005.

Zilberman, Michael. "The Pink Scare." Salon. 29 Feb. 2000. 20 Dec. 2005. www.salon.com/ent/music/feature/2000/02/29/zemfira

Index

7 Days magazine, 81

Agata Kristi (musical group), 72
Akunin, Boris, 80
alcoholism, 33, 35
Alexander III (tsar), 51
All Stars magazine, 81
Andriyanov, Dmitriy, 63
Anna Karenina (Lyev Tolstoy), 80
Aquarium (musical group), 72–73
Arctic Ocean, 34
art, 15, 27, 74
automobiles, 14, 21, 23, 41, 53, 55, 61, 69

ballet, 74–76
Baryshnikov, Mikhail, 75
Beslan, 19
birthdays, 55–56
Black Sea, 79
Bolotin, Andrei, 75
Bolshoi Ballet company, 75
Brodsky, Iosiph, 80–81

Caspian Sea, 79
Caucasus Mountains, 79
cell phones, 23, 38, 60
censorship, 67, 68, 70, 71, 81
Chechen terrorists, 19
Chekhov, Anton, 80
Chernobyl nuclear power plant, 34
Christmas holiday, 13, 45–46
clothing, 17, 23, 27, 41, 65
coastline, 78–79
communications, 37, 38–39
communism, 11–12, 13, 27, 52, 83
country homes, 24, 25
CSKA Moscow soccer team, 78
Cyrillic alphabet, 50

dacha (country homes), 24, 25
Day Watch (film), 69
Declaration of Russian Sovereignty, 52–53
Defender of the Fatherland Day, 46–47
DJ Groove (disc jockey), 73
dnevnik (notebook), 14
doctors, 32, 64–65
Dostoevsky, Fyodor, 80
drinking water, 33, 34
drinks, 13, 28–29, 31, 35, 70

Easter holiday, 49–50
economy, 17, 38, 60, 64, 83
education
    ballet schools, 75–76
    breaks, 13, 16
    class periods, 13
    communism and, 13
    competitions, 17
    dress code, 17
    individuality and, 12–13
    lunch time, 13
    misbehavior, 14
    post-graduate schools, 18
    private schools, 17
    prom night, 18
    public schools, 17
    quarter system, 13
    school days, 12–18
    specialized schools, 13, 16, 17
    syllabus, 13
    universities, 9, 18
employment, 22, 23, 25, 38, 41, 59–62, 63–64, 64–65, 83

Fabergé, Peter Carl, 51
families, 21–22, 24, 28, 31, 32, 33, 38, 39–40, 41, 43, 44,
    48, 52, 53, 54, 56–57, 61, 79. *See also* people.
farming, 16, 24, 25, 61
fast food, 30, 83
Fedorov, Sergei, 77
festivals, 43, 80, 83
flag, 52
foods, 13, 16, 24, 28, 29, 30, 31, 33, 43, 45–46,
    47–48, 50, 52, 55, 59, 70, 83
Fursenko, Andrei, 12

Girl's Tears magazine, 81
glasnost, 12, 67
Gorbachev, Mikhail, 12
Gordeyeva, Yekaterina, 77
Grandfather Frost, 44
Grebenshikov, Boris, 72

health care, 31–32
holidays, 43, 44, 45–46, 47, 49, 52–53, 83
house music, 73
housing, 16, 21–22, 23

imeniny (Saint's day), 56
Independence Day. *See* Russia Day.
International Womens' Day, 46, 49
Internet, 12, 38
Islamic religion, 27–28
Ivanushki International (musical group), 73

jobs. *See* employment.

KGB (Soviet police agency), 71
Kobakhidze, Nelli, 75
Kroshka-Kartoshka restaurants, 30
kulich (dessert), 50
kutya (porridge), 45–46
kvartirniki (concerts), 71

landmass, 9
languages, 13, 17
Last Bell ceremony, 17
literacy rate, 17
literature, 69, 71, 79–81
livestock, 61
Lokomotiv Moscow soccer team, 78
Lukyanenko, Sergei, 69

mafiya (organized crime), 60, 80
magazines, 79, 81, 83
Magnitizdat (musical underground), 71
Makarova, Natalya, 75
maps
    land use, 62
    population density, 22
    topographical, 78

Maria (tsarina), 51
Marinina, Aleksandra, 80
McDonald's restaurants, 30, 83
military, 22, 47, 62–63
Mineral'nye Vody mineral springs, 79
mirrors, 57
Moscow, 15, 16, 23, 34, 51, 53, 59, 65, 70
Moscow Metro, 15, 16
Moscow River, 34
Moscow State University, 9
movies, 67, 68–70, 71
Mumiy Troll (musical group), 71–72
music, 48, 67, 70–73, 83

national holidays, 13, 44, 45
"New Russians," 23, 59
New Year's Day, 44
Night Watch (film), 69
Novoslobodskaya metro station, 15
nuclear power, 34

Olympic Games, 77

Pancake Day, 44, 47–48
Pavlova, Anna, 75
Peace Throughout the World (mosaic), 15
Pelevin, Viktor, 80
Penza, 17
people. *See also* families.
    births, 33, 41, 53
    chores, 25, 41
    deaths, 56–57
    health, 31–33, 34, 35
    leisure time, 22–23, 24, 37, 67, 68, 69, 78–79
    life expectancy, 33
    pregnancies, 33
    vacations, 78–79
Peter the Great (tsar), 52
pirozhki (pie), 29, 83
pollution, 33, 34
Popov, Aleksandr, 77
population, 9
Premier Liga (Premier League), 76, 78
propaganda movies, 68
Protestant Church, 27
Pushkin, Aleksandr, 80

religion, 26–28, 49, 57
"rocka-pops" (musical style), 72

Roman Catholicism, 27–28
Russia Day, 44, 52–53
Russian Orthodox Church, 26–27, 49, 57
Russian Pro Hockey League, 78
Russkoe Bistro restaurants, 30

salaries, 64–65, 83
science-fiction books, 80
secondary schools, 9, 17
Sharapova, Maria, 77
Snow Maiden, 44
soccer, 76, 78
Soviet Union, 11, 12, 13, 23, 27, 38, 49, 52, 53, 62, 68, 71, 72, 80–81
sports, 76, 77, 78
St. Petersburg, 23, 59, 70
St. Valentine's Day, 44, 47
Stalin, Joseph, 15
Strugatsky, Arkady, 80
Strugatsky, Boris, 80
Superleague, 78

t.A.T.u. (musical group), 71, 74
tea, 28–29
teachers, 11, 12, 14, 16, 17, 19, 65
terrorism, 19
toasting, 16, 35, 44, 83
Tolstoy, Lyev, 80
Trans-Siberian Railroad, 51
transportation, 14, 15, 16, 21, 65
Turishcheva, Lyudmila, 77

Union of Soviet Socialist Republics (U.S.S.R.). *See* Soviet Union.

Velikiy Ustug, 44
vocational schools, 9, 17–18, 59
vodka, 35
Volga River, 16, 34
Vysshaya Liga, 78

War and Peace (Lyev Tolstoy), 80
weddings, 53–55
women, 27, 33, 35, 41, 46, 49, 63–64
World War II, 55

Yatsenko, Anastasia, 75

zakuski (hors d'oeuvres), 16, 28
Zemfira (musician), 74

BFT
2/24/11

About the Author
Jessica Smith

Jessica Smith was born in the small town of Chaffee, New York. She studied at the State University of New York at Fredonia before attending Minnesota State University for graduate work in creative writing. Currently she is at work writing her first collection of short stories. She teaches writing at the University at Buffalo.

About the Content Adviser
Natalia Olshanskaya, Ph.D.

Our content adviser for *Teens in Russia*, Natalia Olshanskaya, was born and raised in the former Soviet Union. She is currently an associate professor of Russian, teaching Russian language and literature at Kenyon College in Ohio.

Image Credits